DIVINE

PROMOTION

DIVINE

PROMOTION

"When Promotion Calls Your Name"

Evangelist Mark Dunfee

III

Dedication

I dedicate this book to all of the people who have ev-

er dreamed about being in the ministry. Nobody

knows your name now, but all of that is going to

change soon. God knows your name and that is

enough. Stay faithful in the sheepfold because it

leads to a crown. The little thing you are doing

right now is seen by the One whose eyes are on the

sparrow. Promotion is going to call your name.

When He calls, say, "Here am I, Lord. Send me."

You will never be sorry that you listened to His

voice.

Contents

VIII

Acknowledgments

I would like to thank my youngest daughter, Markie, for countless hours editing and formatting this book. Her wise counsel on things like chapter titles and presentation is the reason that this book has excellence. Her work on this—and many other projects—is priceless.

My son-in-law, Jose, is invaluable in every part of this ministry. Specifically: in the design, the structure, and the printing of this book.

My daughter Billie actually played a major role too in being the architect of the cover. Billie is an intricate part of everything that we are called to do. Billie is a very wise counselor to me. (So is Jose, her husband. He is another son to me.)

All of my kids have a special anointing to take an idea that Dad has and to bring it to life.

I want to thank my wife, Debbie, who has touched my life more than anyone else ever has except Jesus. Debbie believes in me and believes that we can do great things for *God's glory*. Deb and my family are always by my side. My wife and children are the greatest ministry that Jesus ever has privileged me to have.

Introduction

God is a God of process. A God of patterns and cycles. When God wants to *bless you big*, He will often do a little thing in your life. Never despise the day of small things in your life. God is taking you somewhere. He can take you anywhere from nowhere. Believe me, I know. The heart of the Father is looking for those to bless.

Oh, the glorious day in Israel when the temple was dedicated. The crowds at Jerusalem were so massive that in order for the King to be seen, a brazen scaffold was built. As the King knelt on bended knee and cried toward Heaven, the fire of God fell. Everyone could

see and hear the King, and that which fol-
lowed, because the brazen scaffold lifted him
up on high.

Let your life be the brazen scaffold that the
King of *kings* stands upon. The higher that you
are, the higher the Lord Jesus can be seen and
heard.

When I was starting my work for the Lord,
older preachers rarely used the term "going
into the ministry." They certainly *never* spoke
of it as a vocation either. In reference to the
ministry, they only ever talked about how they
answered the "*call*." I never heard one of them
say that they regretted it. Never. You never
will either.

Someone is looking for you. Someone is
going to find you. It's divine promotion.

Divine promotion is going to call out your name.

Oh, how God needs you and wants to *bless* you. Remember those who came before you and those who come after you—that we all may rejoice together in that great day of the Lord's *harvest*.

Do you not say, it is still four months until harvest time comes? Look! I tell you, raise your eyes and observe the fields and see how they are already white for harvesting. (John 4:35 AMPC)

There is a field for you that has your name on it, and it will bring you so much *joy*. Incredible joy.

1

The Kingdom of Relationships

God is going to promote you so that He can use you in an even greater way. The purpose of God's blessing in your life is so that He can use you to advance His Kingdom. God wants to make you great in His Kingdom and make you a person of great influence for God's glory.

The Rich Fool in the Bible

Then he told them a story: "A rich man had a fertile farm that produced fine crops. He said to himself, 'What should I do? I don't have room for all my crops.' Then he said, 'I know! I'll tear down my barns and build bigger ones. Then I'll have room enough to store all my wheat and other goods. And I'll sit back and say to myself, "My friend, you have enough stored away for years to come. Now take it easy! Eat, drink, and be merry!"' But God said to him, 'You fool! You will die this very night. Then who will get everything you worked for?' Yes, a person is a fool to store up earthly wealth but not have a rich relationship with God." (Luke 12:16-21 NLT)

I sincerely wonder what God thinks of the idle American culture of laying up enough money so that you can just sit around and retire and do nothing, especially for God. As Billy Graham said, "There is nothing about retirement in the Bible."

God doesn't care if you have multiplied millions, but He sure wants you to keep a wonderful relationship with your loving Heavenly Father. Always be rich toward God with your money and with whatever else the Father puts within your hand. Prosperity for a purpose is a tremendous blessing. Earthly wealth and temporal positions that make us proud and turn us away from God are not a blessing at all. Even if you are president of the United States, you won't be there for long.

If you are position-oriented then you will never be happy or satisfied, but will always be craving and lusting after a greater position. *If you think a position alone without relationships will make you happy, it is not true.*

Success is not a position. True, meaningful success is always rooted and grounded in meaningful relationships. If I am a *zillionaire* and the star founder of the greatest company on earth but have no relationship with Jesus Christ, am I really successful? If my kids hate me even though I have a magnificent position, and my wife doesn't want to be around me, how blessed am I? A position with no one to share it with is a lonely and barren planet to live on.

Love Is Not Jealous

In the carnal world, men and women fight and duel each other for position and authority in companies, and sad to say, sometimes even in the Church. It is brutal and it is not of God. It is a million miles away from the *love of God*, and the *fruit of the Spirit*, of which there are nine (Galatians 5:22-23).

In the Kingdom of God, there are *more than enough blessings for everyone to be promoted and used in a great way!* When you start wanting others to be promoted and to be blessed, then God is getting ready to use you. In fact, some of your most meaningful, joyful, and satisfying ministry times will be seeing people around you promoted and prospered and knowing you played a part.

No one has to be demoted for you to be promoted on high. The better that someone else does, the more blessed and incredibly happy you are. When you have that kind of spirit and truly love people, and desire that they be *blessed by God*, it all comes back to you. Not only do you want to see Jesus bless them but you are willing to do everything that you can do to help them get ahead.

There should never be any bit of a dog-eat-dog mentality among people of faith. In honor we prefer one another (Romans 12:10), and speak well of one another (James 4:11). The essence and the foundation of these kinds of eternal relationships are walking in love one toward another.

Truly, when we are *relationship-oriented* toward God and others, it is a true life-changing mindset. Your promotion and blessing aren't lessened or increased by what someone else does or doesn't have. Maybe you came from a large family and there were only so many biscuits on the table. Or if everyone wanted a certain pie then the slices for everyone were just made smaller and smaller. Or if no one wanted pie or a biscuit then you got more biscuits or a larger slice of pie. God has more than enough bounty and blessings for everybody. Everyone can be full and satisfied and rejoice over the goodness of God that others are experiencing.

If you are in the ministry and your friend's ministry grows and it looks like they are experiencing divine multiplication and supernatural promotion, are you going to sulk and be bitter? Most preachers are pretty good number crunchers when it comes to attendance and crowds. And so many men and women of God lead lonely and isolated lives feeling a neighboring ministry or pastor stole their people and blessing. *Nobody can steal your promotion and blessing.*

In today's world, churches often swap saints instead of winning the lost. Let's just say that someone steals your people (they are not your people; they are God's) and temporarily it looks like you have been done a great wrong. *How you react to it is more important than anything. Our attitude about what has happened to us is far more important than what has happened to us.* You can get wounded and then get bitter and quit. Then you can spend the next twenty years talking about it and letting all who will listen know how unjust people have been to you. That spirit does not lead to promotion, but will keep you small and small-minded. The day you realize that nobody, including the devil, can stop you, and that every child of God can fulfill their destiny, it is a great day. *The favor of God* can't be stopped by man.

> And the patriarchs, moved with envy, sold Joseph into Egypt: but God was with him, and delivered him out of all his afflictions, and gave him favour and wisdom in the sight of Pharaoh king of Egypt; and he made him governor over Egypt and all his house. (Acts 7:9-10)

Divine Relationships

Jesus has a full, rich, and satisfying life for us and for our families. I want to be very close to

God, to all of my family, and to the divine connections that Jesus has put into my life. Doing *the will of God,* and *loving and blessing my family,* is forever. Nothing else is really important in this life or in eternity.

When God wants to *bless your socks off,* He will do it by increasing your relationship with *Him,* and by bringing what I call "divine connections" or "divine relationships" into your life.

So many people are not willing to have a loving relationship for some reason with the God who adores them. So they labor on in the strength of their self-effort, by the sweat of their brow, like a fallen Adam just thrown out of the Garden of Eden. But in the New Testament or the *New Covenant,* God's strength is our strength, and we are *seated with Christ in heavenly places.* We go in His *power* and in the *name of Jesus*, that name that is above every other name in Heaven and on earth.

It is not our ability and self-worthiness that promotes us. It is our relationship with the King of Kings. *We are loved and known by the Father* so we can risk loving other people. The *blessing of the Lord that maketh rich and adds no sorrow* is on us so that we never lack (Proverbs 10:22). We are in love with God and *loved by God*. If we miss it, He loves us and will forgive us when we ask and repent. He will always do us good and never do us bad. If something is not going right in your life, it is the enemy and not your Heavenly *Father* trying to do or put something on you. *God is good all the time.*

Standing by a little mailbox on a cold September morning, when I was 12 I waited for the school bus for 7th grade to arrive. It was then that I noticed a cute little 11 year old girl.

In my wildest dreams I never could have known or even wildly imagined how that relationship would joyously and forever change my life.

Debbie was that cute little girl and today is my cute little blond-haired wife and best friend. What an amazing and beautiful woman the little girl has become. I believe in *divine relationships.*

As a 14 year old boy, I left an altar with tears in my eyes after a Sunday night service and had a forever changed life because my relationship with God had changed. If Jesus ever calls you into the ministry—go. *Just go.* Drop your fishing nets and follow him. You will always be glad that you did.

I answered the call of God and have never been sorry that I went. God has promoted me far beyond all that I could ever ask, think, or dream. And it is just the beginning. *He has made me glad* and He will do the same for you.

Jesus told me that I would influence a whole new generation of preachers and maybe you are one of them. *God is going to set you on high,* even though you may start your ministry in a lowly place.

I am humbled by the blessing of God in my life and in all of my family. I certainly am not of the mindset that it is because of me or that I deserve it. When I went to that old-fashioned altar I thought that I was giving everything up. Oh, how wrong I was about that. I am so glad that I answered His call. I didn't realize it at the time, but *promotion* was calling my name.

2

Passing the Money Test

The love of money is the root of all evil (1 Timothy 6:10). It makes people wander from the faith the Bible teaches us and pierces them through with many sorrows.

Most people that I have seen God really promote have plenty of money and access to it at all times. But even though they have lots of money, *money doesn't have them*. They make money work for them as their servant, and as good stewards are constantly giving it away for Kingdom purposes, which actually gives them a constant flow of even more money. Yet how often I have witnessed those who cling to the little that they have, and though they constantly promote themselves, they never really rise. It is as though the few shekels that they have, has them right by the throat. The steady and constant fearful thoughts of losing the little that they have keeps them from being faithful givers. So the very thing that they fear comes upon them like a modern-day Job.

For us to be really and truly *blessed*, there needs to be a *divine activation* of *supernatural increase* in our lives and in our families. I think that every one of us want much more than a paycheck-to-paycheck sub-existence of struggle. It will not be that way anymore in your life when promotion calls your name. But for that to happen and for you to reap and keep on earth and in eternity, you will have to pass the money test.

You pass the money test by how you deal with a little bit of money.

Oh, I have heard grand proclamations of people saying if they suddenly won the lottery then they would do this or that. *If people are not faithful with a little money, it is unlikely that they will be faithful with a lot of money.*

When God gives you seed and you do not sow it, you are setting yourself up for perpetual lack, which is to be avoided like the plague.

2 Corinthians 9:10 reveals that God gives seed *to the sower*. Have you ever heard people say that they have nothing to give? If you ever

hear that, it is a proclamation that they are not givers. God gives seed to people who have made giving and sowing a lifestyle. Then they receive more and more seed which becomes more and more harvest.

How to Have a Worldwide Famine

Can you imagine if for several years all of the farmers of the earth just quit planting and sowing seed? If no one on our planet worked their fields and took the first steps of sowing seeds which bring a harvest?

Think of it: if no grain was grown, no vegetables planted, and all of the earth just kept eating the stores of seed that individuals and nations have, it wouldn't be long and the whole wide world would be turned upside down with starvation and hunger.

It is not an overstatement to say that if the world stopped sowing barley, wheat, and soybeans, the planet would be propelled toward famine. Soon there would be absolutely nothing more important than the harvest.

Newscasters would stand beside fields of earthly soil and ask to interview those who work the ground. The cable news networks would have lead stories and 24-hour coverage of the coming harvest. Life on earth would depend upon it.

For the world to survive, someone has to plant seed and tend it faithfully until it is multiplied to feed all of us so that we can all live. I do not believe, though, that we are going to have to go through that. Even unregenerate mankind believes in sowing natural seed, because if it was not planted, we would starve.

> While the earth remaineth, seedtime and harvest, and cold and heat, and summer and winter, and day and night shall not cease. (Genesis 8:22)

Never let the enemy trick you into not caring about the Godly process of sowing and reaping which yields the harvest.

Some Christians say, "Oh, we just need a little, and none of us care at all about earthly and temporal things." That has a certain sound of dignity to it, but *it is a spirit of poverty clothed in religious rags.*

Churches are not built, and wonderful, Godly causes pushed forward, if no one cares.

What if you believed God for more money to help your family and your church? Or a Bible school student or young person just starting out in the ministry? What if you blessed the Gospel veteran who won your whole family to Jesus, or bought Gospel literature, or helped a missionary?

When you realize that the money God entrusts to you is not your own but belongs to Heaven, *then you have passed the money test.*

Does this mean that you can never have a nice vacation or enjoy the blessing of the Lord? Of course not! God is so much more kind and generous than anyone who walks upon the face of the earth.

> ... the living God, who giveth us richly
> all things to enjoy. (1 Timothy 6:17)

Help Your Children Pass the Money Test

Blessing your children and even your children's children is biblical and a reflection of the *Father's heart.*

> A good man leaveth an inheritance to his children's children: and the wealth of the sinner is laid up for the just. (Proverbs 13:22)

Setting your children up so that they can be a *supernatural blessing* is one of the greatest gifts you can give them. When you teach and model *sowing and reaping with an expectancy of a great harvest,* you have blessed them forever.

Money with an eternal purpose attached to it is a mighty river of *God's grace*. Be a big part of that eternal river by passing the money test. The more that you sow, the more that you will reap.

> Give, and [gifts] will be given to you; good measure, pressed down, shaken together, and running over, will they pour into [the pouch formed by] the bosom [of your robe and used as a bag]. For with the measure you deal out [with the measure you use when you confer benefits on others], it will be measured back to you. (Luke 6:38 AMPC)

You will be glad that you passed the test

here in this life and in the world to come. You and your family will always be *blessed* in all things on this earth. And in the land where angels stand before the throne of God, you will be forever humble and eternally thankful that you passed *the money test*.

3

The Lifestyle Called Blessed

We are not blessed so that we never have to go back to the ditch. We are blessed so that we have the means to minister. The donkey that God gave you is so that you can carry the wounded. The money that God gives you is so you can buy and pour out the wine and oil that brings healing.

The day that you stop loving the wounded that lie in the ditch, you are not really blessed. You have just joined the religious crowd that acts like it cannot see and walks on by what Jesus Christ loves and died for.

Why should one be promoted? Promotion is not about getting a new position so that we can feel good about ourselves. It is not about making more money so that we can just have a life of ease; promotion is so that you and I can change the world and make an eternal difference for eternity.

God Is a Promoter

For promotion cometh neither from the east, nor from the west, nor from the south. (Psalm 75:6)

True promotion comes only from God. Your self-effort may help you attain a man-made promotion, but it will not bring peace into your life, and the position likely will not last. A life attained and maintained by self is not, in any way, comparable to the joy that comes from walking in the favor of God. A sacrificed marriage, family, health, and shattered nerves are the price people pay for promoting themselves. Faith walks through doors that God opens, and walks through them with peace. Stress is not one of the gifts of the Spirit.

When you flow in what God has called you to do, it is a wonderful life of loving what you do. There is much joy in laboring in the fields of the Lord. You will never be sorry that you did the will of God. The longer you do the will of God, the more joyful and the more satisfaction you have. Sorrow and regret are the fruit of a wasted life. *Blessed* is a wonderful lifestyle and is available to every believer. And blessing you gives God pleasure.

> Let the Lord be magnified, who takes pleasure in the prosperity of His serv-ant. (Psalm 35:27 AMPC)

Bring the Blessing to a Ditch

One of the most famous stories in the Bible involves a wounded man lying on the side of the road in a ditch (Luke 10:30). This story tells us a whole lot about what God is looking for and how He wants us to be.

I hope you've never been in the ditch, but if you ever are, pray that a Good Samaritan comes by your way. And if you have never helped anyone get up out of the ditch, you need to. Heaven is calling. Not to gates of splendor, but to the highways and byways of earth. Rescuing hurting people is what Jesus taught and lived by. It is the way of the twelve. While preachers parse Greek verbs, a world is lost and going to Hell. In the shadow of the steeple are crying people.

Gladly follow the path that Jesus has for your life. You will find that it is a good and a glorious path. But if that path never leads you to a ditch to help a hurting person Christ died for, you are off track.

When ministers try to climb the high pinnacles to be seen and praised by man, the enemy comes. When God exalts a man or woman, or a nation, everything about it is different. When you try to exalt yourself, it is a dangerous precipice beside a bottomless pit.

Loving the Unlovable

Jesus loved the people no one else loved. Love God by loving people that He loves. Ask God to give you a special love for people that can do nothing for you in the natural.

If you were a despised tax collector raising money for the occupying Romans, Jesus would come to your house to eat. If you were a sinful woman, Jesus would keep you from being stoned. For the leper that no one else would even come near, Jesus had a touch which turned to healing. The lower and the sicker and the more despised that you were by man and religion, the more Jesus loved you. Some things, especially this, has never changed and it never will. The love of Jesus went into ditches to love people that no one else could have cared less about.

There is a "spa-for-the-saved" mentality that has crept into way too many of our churches. A backsliding people that call themselves Christian but do not love or have compassion for sinners is a church that has lost its way. They are the lost elder brother of the prodigal son who was lost. You can be at *Father's house* and not have the heart of the Father for the prodigals gone astray.

The lower that you are willing to go to help the hurting of humanity, the higher that Heaven will promote you.

God is always looking for someone to promote. Most of the people that *God* has promoted were found in the ditch; either lying in the ditch themselves or helping some other wounded soul climb out.

God promotes people who have compassion for those inside and outside of the Church. I want to love what God loves and to be stirred by that which stirs the heart of God.

Do You Really Want to Be Happy?

How can someone really be happy if they never help anyone? Jumping in church and singing happy songs is great, but if we always want to receive a blessing but never want to give one, we are mistaken. That is not why we are blessed by the Father. We are not given money just so we can bank it all, having no ministry attached to it. That is not really being blessed. That isn't to say I believe that God is against investment portfolios, saving, and investing. Long-term faith involves generational thinking. It expects Jesus to come tonight but plans as if He might tarry for a hundred years.

Real faith sets up the next generation by teaching them to pray and to walk in the Holy Ghost. It teaches them to be good stewards. It blesses their grandchildren, the generation after that, and even the one after that.

My grandmother influenced my grandchildren just as much as if she had lunch with them every day. By God's grace all of her great-great-grandchildren are serving Jesus. She didn't leave me a lot of money, but she and my grandfather left me *faith*. With that faith I can get all things.

Again, I am not against great wealth and

passing it on. Abraham, Isaac, Jacob, Joseph, and Ephraim certainly were not against it. Neither is God. But when the Lord Jesus blesses you, remember the poor and remember the work of the Gospel. Teach your blessed children and all of their descendants to do the same.

A lifestyle called blessed reaches out to the hurting. It is *prosperity with a purpose* that matters for all of time and eternity.

Jesus wants to set us all free from the selfish mindset that is in the world and has even crept into the Church today. We are *blessed to be a blessing*. We are *saved to serve,* and when that is the reason that we want money, then we will never, ever lack. That's what I call *blessed.*

4

It's Mercy Time

Mercy will get real important in your life if you ever need it. The best way to make sure you have mercy if you ever need it is to always show it to others. Mercy is God's love in action to people who don't deserve it, and many times, do not even expect it. When the Holy Spirit leads your life, He will lead you on a path of mercy that none of us can ever earn or deserve. *God's leading is a merciful leading.*

Remember, the mercy we show someone else may just be the vaccine which helps us from making the same blunder someone else has made. I'd rather err on the side of mercy than be a legalistic Pharisee. There are more than enough "Stone the Fallen" ministries, and far fewer "Woman at the Well' outreaches in the merciful name of Jesus.

Saints That Stone Other Saints

Never become hard-hearted. Have you ever notice how *hard-hearted* some preachers have become? They are the blind leading the blind of whom Jesus spoke. They don't know it, but they are in a religious ditch, and they have led millions astray.

Years ago, I heard about a preacher's son who got his girlfriend pregnant. Many preachers from all around came to a sort of judgment tribunal. The young couple were bitterly treated and were verbally stoned. Had they sinned? Yes. The young couple had made a mistake, and the stones flew that night at God's house. They were religiously thrown by those who were not without sin in their own lives. Everyone was in the ditch. And seemingly everyone did their best to bury the young couple alive. It was a night to remember. A night of no mercy.

Not too many executioners get promoted. If they ever are lifted up a little bit, their faces are usually covered by a religious mask like someone who did executions in the dark ages.

Mercy doesn't have to wear a mask. It will look you in the face with eyes of love.

The older I have become, the more God's mercy has entered into my spirit. The higher Jesus has lifted up our ministry and the more exposure that we have, the more I love sinners. If you don't have mercy that flows like a mighty river in your life, then you can expect to sit on *God's back shelf* for a long time. Never forget that God Almighty can lift you up real quick, but without God's mercy pride can bring you down real quick.

Whenever God uses you a little or lifts you up a little, be quick to give Jesus all the glory. Fleshly pride will put a carnal edge to your personality that shouldn't be there. It will make you compete with God's other children instead of being wholeheartedly glad and thankful they are being blessed. *Until you are glad and truly happy about someone else's promotion and blessing, you are not really ready to be promoted yourself.*

Humbly ask God to keep selfish pride out of your life. The more our Heavenly Father promotes and blesses you, the more you praise Him and thank God for *grace*.

Foolish pride will set you on the back shelf like the pickles at Grandma's house that have an old expiration date. I have sadly seen people who at one time did great exploits for God, and pride embalmed their ministry and usefulness.

God Is Greater Than Your Failure

If not for God's grace, it could be me and you. God doesn't give up on people and neither should we. Maybe you have failed the Lord Jesus and missed the mark by sin. It's not too late for God to use you. How often I have seen people with epic failures in their lives get back on track and be used mightily by God because of grace.

There are not too many people who are perfect and have always had perfect track records to man the sails on the ship called *The Church.* Had most of us gotten what we deserved instead of what grace affords, we would have been thrown overboard and swallowed by a whale like Jonah.

We are not the judges of who God uses.

I have actually seen self-righteous people who thought it was their ministry to decide and judge who God should use and who God should promote. Then they would get mad and start to walk a bitter highway if God lifted someone up that—for some reason—didn't meet with their approval.

Some preachers of the Gospel let themselves get angry. They stay constantly agitated and upset because God used someone they deemed unworthy. More than likely, these same people would have had a pretty bad attitude with Jesus using Saul of Tarsus who became the *Apostle Paul*. I have decided to mind my own business and to let God do the choosing and promoting. I will rejoice and be glad that the Gospel of *peace* is preached.

Now unto him that is able to keep you from falling, and to present you faultless before the presence of his glory with exceeding joy. (Jude 1:24)

God Promotes Humble People

Pride will bring you down real quick just like it did lucifer. *Humble people end up with God exalting them.* You won't have to manipulate or step on somebody for Jesus to lift up your ministry. It will just happen. It is far better to be humble before God in private and then let Him lift you up publicly. Without God's grace, the opposite can also happen to us. The hand that lifts you up is also able to keep you from falling.

When you start really loving people that *Christ died for,* it is an inward sign that the Lord is going to start using you like never before. *Religion will teach you to pass some people by because they don't measure up.* Religion has a lot of measurements that aren't founded on the Bible.

5

The Surprising People Who Will

Get You Promoted

D on't waste your life trying to politically connect with those who look like they could promote you in the natural and through the strength of the flesh. It is unnecessary and almost always a waste of time.

The people God is going to use to promote you

most likely can do nothing for you. Most people wouldn't waste a breath or a dollar on them, but they will change you and your family's lives forever. What you do and what you try to do for them will change you and yours forever.

I know what it is like to spend a lot of sweat and effort chasing after the impressive. Then blessed Jesus had me start *loving the un-lovable.* My life now is a testimony that *when you love the people that nobody else loves, God will connect you to people that everybody would like to be connected to.* Your life will be too.

You see, *everybody is somebody to Jesus.* Soon after I started loving people that even the Church had passed by, I heard promotion calling my name. For so long I longed and tried so hard to impress the impressive. *Then one glorious day by God's great grace,* I started flowing in a love for people that was not my own.

44

Oh, what a happy day when I started only really caring about what God thinks about me and stopped agonizing over what the self-righteous and religious think. It changed my whole life forever. *Peace—the kind of peace that surpasses all understanding—came to live at my house.* I'm never going back to that old way of life.

When peace came to live at my house, the doorbell rang and *the favor of God* moved in to stay. They were both sent by *promotion,* and my whole life and family have never been the same. *God gave me the blessing that I had always longed for and could not contain.*

God promotes people who love the wounded and suffering. A lack of compassion almost always means a permanent demotion in the Kingdom of God until you get some God-given compassion.

God Promotes Compassionate People

True compassion has to do something, and it almost always is for someone who can do little or nothing for you in return.

True compassion is loving what God loves and reaching out to a broken and sinful place called Earth. God's compassion does something about the suffering that it sees. Religion just walks on by.

I used to be religious, but by God's grace I have sensed and felt the compassion of the Lord Jesus Christ. I never, ever want it to leave me.

In my early ministry I would judge you. I was so unhappy. But *Christ's mighty love* wrapped His strong arms around me. His goodness will not let me go. His compassion within helps me to say, *"But for the grace of God, there go I."* Now I have peace within. It started when, by God's *grace,* I started loving the wounded and suffering.

God has made me a happy man. You can be happy too. Jesus taught me how to be happy. Let these words of the compassionate Savior teach you how to have a wonderful, *blessed,* and *happy life:*

See What Others Ignore and Walk By

Jesus replied with a story: "A Jewish man was traveling from Jerusalem down to Jericho, and he was attacked by bandits. They stripped him of his clothes, beat him up, and left him half dead beside the road. By chance a

47

priest came along. But when he saw the man lying there, he crossed to the other side of the road and passed him by." (Luke 10:30-31 NLT)

Why didn't the priest stop and help the wounded man suffering in the ditch? It was because he didn't care. The quickened pace of the priest's steps could be seen and heard as he passed the precious man lying wounded by the side of the road.

Ancient Jericho was a priestly city. Some scholars say that no less than 12,000 priests lived there. It was filled with priests who would frequently walk the Jericho Road to minister in the temple at Jerusalem.

The "pastor" passed him by. It's easy to get so busy in the temple that you forget about the ditches where the sinful and suffering lie. He walked on toward his appointment.

Soon the temple assistant, a Levite, saw the wounded man in the ditch. Guess what? He passed him by too.

Church is not just for "church people" but for the hurting who need Jesus.

The people you help get up out of the ditch may be the key to your future.

"Then a despised Samaritan came along, and when he saw the man, he felt compassion for him. Going over to him, the Samaritan soothed his wounds with olive oil and wine and bandaged them. Then he put the man on his own donkey and took him to an inn, where he took care of him. The next day he handed the innkeeper two silver coins, telling him, 'Take care of this man. If his bill runs higher than this, I'll pay you the next time I'm here.' Now which of these three would you say was a neighbor to the man who was attacked by bandits?" Jesus asked. The man replied, "The one who showed him mercy." Then Jesus said, "Yes, now go and do the same." (Luke 10:33-37 NLT)

Real ministry is in the ditch where a lot of God's people refuse to go.

The call to the ditch where the wounded lie still reverberates throughout the ages to the Church today. A call to the suffering. The outcasts of humanity are lying there needing a healing touch. Jesus has never changed His mind about people who are lying in the ditch and suffering. He wants someone to get down in the ditch and help them.

You Haven't Failed Just Because It Looks like You Have

When I was in my late 40s it seemed like every dream I ever had for ministry died. I was a struggling pastor in the inner city of Paterson, New Jersey, right beside New York City. People were staying away from the church by the thousands. Inwardly, I had a craving for success that was insufferable because my view of success was wrong.

Success is doing your assignment and the will of God for your life. It may not look very impressive to some people but it is very impressive to God. I spent years searching in vain for what I already had. I had pleased the Lord Jesus, but there were sure a lot of other people that I had upset.

It seemed the harder I tried to build something that looked impressive to man, the less I accomplished.

A Life-Changing Bowl of Soup

Right in the midst of millions I preached to a scattered little band of believers. I couldn't even pay my bills, and could hardly take care of my four children. *It was then that God showed me the miracle of helping people who had been wounded and had fallen in the ditch.*

I will always remember a certain cold November night I worked in my office and got ready for the prayer meeting that evening at church.

A homeless man knocked on my door, and with just one look, it was evident that he was in the ditch.

The precious man looked like Grizzly Adams from a TV show, and was cold and hungry. I offered him a bowl of soup, and as I started to heat the soup in the microwave, I began to cry.

I got down in the ditch to help someone, and it changed my life and my family's lives forever.

It was as if Jesus in a white robe had knocked on my door that day. Jesus did knock on my door, because the Bible says in Matthew

25:40, "Inasmuch as ye have done it unto one of the least of these my brethren, ye have done it unto me."

Soon I was pastoring people no one else wanted and no one else cared anything about. People with no teeth, old clothes, and who smelled like cigarette smoke came into our church. I watched those who had money leave our church and go away because they didn't realize that *the least of these* was *Jesus* coming to church.

I learned that bias and prejudice can wear a suit and act religious and even try to keep out of *God's house* those who need it most.

Soon I pastored a New Testament church where the ground was level at the foot of the cross, and I had peace. Jesus saved me from a selfish life.

The Rest of the Story

Today, Jericho Road Church is thriving. Literally untold thousands of homeless people have been ministered to. My son, Ben, is the pastor and has taken the church a million miles further than I ever did. It looks soon that there will be Jericho Road Churches all across the nation, helping people that are largely forgotten and ignored. All because years ago we heard someone's cry from the ditch.

I'm glad I got soiled with the sweat, mud, and stains of the suffering. It pulled me up out of the ditch I myself was in. It changed my family for generations to come. Going down into the ditch to help someone else changed my whole ministry. I went from babysitting the saved to serving on the frontlines for God.

Now Debbie and I travel this nation for Jesus and have open doors that no man can shut. The *goodness of God* staggers my imagination. All of my dreams are coming true. I have *joy unspeakable* and my wife, Debbie, and I are standing with our family in a large place of *supernatural prosperity*. What matters most is that eternity is going to be different for untold thousands of people. They will be in Heaven forever and ever instead of forever and ever in Hell.

I've never been sorry that I reached out to the people that Jesus put in my pathway. Oh, the wonderful times that Christ's *amazing love* has whelmed up within me and all of a sudden I could feel great compassion. A compassion that stirred me to action.

Faith will always find a way to do something and be the biggest blessing possible. No one ever gave up from too much faith. Faith will find a way or make a way even when there is no way.

God has a plan for your life and it is a lot bigger than you think. This is not the time for little dreams or for small plans. It is not the time to be so caught up in doing our thing and where we are going that we miss ministry opportunities.

I want to be so close to Jesus that I can hear a whisper from Him in my spirit within. I want to have such a fellowship and friendship with the Lord Jesus that *what God thinks and wants means more to me than anything else.* There is a place in God where the Holy Spirit's still small voice is louder than anything else that you hear or ever have heard. It is *promotion* calling out your name.

6

The Little Thing Done Well

The Kingdom of God is an upside-down kingdom. What you gain you lose, and what it looks like you lose you gain. The way up in the Kingdom is by going down. The way down in the Kingdom is to scratch and claw for the top while stepping on others. You will get further while on your knees than by using sharp elbows. There are enough seats at the King's table of the Lord Jesus Christ for everyone to be honored and *abundantly blessed*. I don't ever have to steal a ministry or put down another precious brother or sister in Christ. I don't ever have to be jealous of anyone anywhere, and neither do you.

God wants to heal every person and bless the socks off every individual, and He longs to give all of His children something important and dynamic to do that is eternal.

The jealous comparison that the enemy of your soul tries to get you to make with someone else is utterly foolish. Comparing yourself to others will always leave you arguing with James, John, and Simon about who is the greatest.

Just run your race with patience in the joy

of the Lord, and your day will soon come. A day of so many blessings that you and your loved ones will be unable to contain them. To do otherwise is to be constantly filled with un-easiness because it looks like somebody else is in the passing lane speeding by.

The little that you are doing (in the eyes of carnal man) may mean more to God than you can ever comprehend.

For who hath despised the day of small things? (Zechariah 4:10)

Be Remembered for Eternity

Many of earth's forgotten people will be remembered forever in eternity. Giants in eternity will be the forgotten missionaries or the little Christian grandmothers who prayed fervently. Ladies who persevered in serving God and never got bitter even though their husband loved alcohol more than them. Many of these giants even won their unsaved husband or wife to Christ. How about the faithful pastor of a little church in a little town that no one else even cares about? Unappreciated and unpaid, they work a job and pay most of the bills of the church so a few children and widows can have a place to worship and pray. Believe me that they will have their day before the judgment seat of Christ, and *great will be their reward.*

A whole lot of people are a whole lot more glamorous to God than they are to man. The glory of man passes away, *but the reward and promotion of the Lord lasts for all of eternity.*

So many people are spending so much of their lives on that which does not really matter all that much. What about you, dear reader, who Jesus helped me to write this book for? Have you done, and are you doing, what Jesus has asked you to do?

It's not too late.

Do what the master calls you to do with a pure and perfect heart. You will be so glad that you did in this life, and in the heavenly life to come. You will have peace of mind, joy, and contentment. The legacy of faith you hand down to your children is going to be priceless and so precious to them and to their children forever and ever.

God will promote you in this life, and when you stand before Jesus you will be so glad you did not waste your life, but instead obeyed God and did what He asked you to do.

My Uncommonly Common Grandfather

My grandfather Dunfee was one of the most successful men that I have ever met. He would laugh to hear me say it and even be embarrassed. The world never knew his name, but God did.

I wouldn't be writing this today if not for the influence of his humble life. Often I see a lot people who are related to my grandfather—even his direct descendants—and although many never met him or are too young to really remember him, he changed their lives forever.

Grace was his favorite subject. He didn't

have great talent or obvious natural ability that would impress you, but Grampie did the best he could with what God gave him to work with. He ran his race, and the New York Times certainly never mentioned it when his earthly race was won. But that somewhat short and humble State-of-Mainer—along with my precious grandmother by his side—sure affected a lot of people.

He was born in 1913, and the ripple effect of his life continues to roll outward in this life and for all eternity. Like I said, he was one of the most successful men that I ever knew, although Grampie likely would laugh to hear me say it. *He did his assignment. He did what he could.* He was faithful to God's house, paid his tithes, and kept his family in church. He forgave and forgot, and did the little thing well.

As a result, and because of God's great

grace, all of Grampie Dunfee's children, grand-children, great-grandchildren, and a small army of great-great-grandchildren are all serving Jesus and have been washed in the blood. All that are old enough, by God's grace, are serving Jesus.

Many of his grandchildren and great-grandchildren are in full-time ministry. Many others are on their way to fulfilling the *CALL OF GOD* on their lives. Most of them never met him or barely remember him, but I met him and I sure remember him; and I surely will meet him again. Grampie Dunfee was an uncommon common man.

What about you has the devil told you? That your little job doesn't matter and that no one knows your name? Heaven knows your name. The little thing that you do matters to God, and it sure matters to your future. You will also likely find out, in this life and in the life to come, that it mattered to a whole lot more people than you would ever think.

God's Will at Your Fingertips

Whatever your hand finds to do, do it with all your might. (Ecclesiastes 9:10 AMPC)

Your next assignment is usually the one that is right in front of you. It may not be glamorous and it may not be something to brag to your friends about, but do it gladly for Jesus.

In fact, nothing we do is something that we should brag to our friends about. We have nothing to brag about in and of ourselves. The grace of Jesus gives us the talent, the opportunities and open doors, and the favor of God. All of the bragging needs to be about Jesus. The longer I live the more clearly I see that God uses me in spite of me and certainly not because I deserve it or earned it.

When I was 18 or 19 years old, I had an opportunity to work for about a week at my home church. It was a part of my Bible school training. My pastor was a handsome man and one of the most prominent ministers in all of New England. People knew his name and he influenced hundreds of preachers. He had a TV ministry that touched thousands of people, and at the height of his ministry pastored well over 500 people. He was loved and respected and it seemed that everyone everywhere knew who he was.

So many times he received offers and

opportunities to go to bigger cities and bigger places. It was impressive to watch him preach and see the success he had, especially if you were a young preacher like me, just starting out and really wanting to be used by God in a very special way.

I remember the first day my cousin and I came to work at the house of the Lord (for the Bible school training). I had envisioned us riding around with him doing something glamorous. Maybe holding a microphone for him or even doing a little bit of talking on the TV program. I could see us on the church platform making announcements, leading in prayer, or even preaching a sermon. Maybe some hospital visits or even anything at all that spoke of our progress. I know that I certainly longed to do something exciting. I was hungry to take another step in my advancement and progress on the ministerial ladder of success. But God and my pastor had a few different ideas.

One morning, my pastor showed us a vacuum cleaner and had us lugging chairs and tables around. No one seemed to want to use our many other skills and talents that week. Coffee breaks and trips to the restaurant were also not as frequent as I wanted them to be.

It was in the fall of the year, and winter always comes to the state of Maine. I remember one day when my pastor led my cousin and I out behind the church. He told us to take long, thin pieces of wood called "lathes" and nail them to the bottom of the church building. But before we nailed them, we were to make sure that a big piece of plastic was under the wood being nailed to the side of the building. Then we were to stretch out the plastic and wrap it over a bale of hay. After this we put a two-by-four piece of wood or some rocks on the ground to hold the other end of the plastic. Then we would repeat the very unglamorous process as we went down the length of the building.

So here I was standing out back of the church building with my cousin, where no one would ever see me doing a very menial task that would help keep the church warm during the coming freezing winter storms. In New England, the old timers called it banking the house. In fact, all we did that whole week was manual labor. It seemed that my back was needed a lot more than my voice.

I never have forgotten that week. God used it to give a little well-needed dose of humility. I learned to obey my pastor and do the assignment that was set before me. I learned that I needed to keep my feet on the ground, and that *serving is what God's ministry is all about*. The day that you stop serving is the day that you probably have left God's best plan for your life.

My pastor was so very good to me. Many times he had me preach for him and I know in his heart that he loved me and was proud of me. I know that I loved him and was proud of him.

Early in his ministry, in his 20s, he would work all night at a factory. Then he would go to the little Pentecostal Mission and all day long, by himself, paint the church, climbing up and down a ladder or scaffolding. No wonder he didn't feel sorry for me doing a few hours of labor. I'm glad now that he didn't feel sorry for me and just try to make my flesh feel good.

If you can't do a little thing well for God, then

you may never get the opportunity to do something big.

I get to go so many places and get to do so many things that I certainly don't deserve, and never could have earned. Had I known how good God was getting ready to be to me and my family, I would have laughed all the while that I ran the vacuum cleaner.

Friend, trust me, you can start laughing right now ahead of time.

Anything you do for Christ with a pure heart is not done in vain. It is *so worth it,* both in this life and in the life to come, to *do the little thing well.*

Then after you have done that, do another little thing well for Jesus; and do another little thing again and again. Do it just because you love Jesus.

Therefore, my beloved brethren, be ye stedfast, unmoveable, always abounding in the work of the Lord, forasmuch as ye know that your labour is not in vain in the Lord. (1 Corinthians 15:58)

I still miss my pastor and think of him almost every day. Many of the precious people that he ministered to are in Heaven. He is waiting for me there and will meet me and a lot of others at that "meeting in the air," when Jesus comes to take His children home in the rapture of the Church. I think that he would be pleased with what I am doing. Someday when I see him again, I will thank him for teaching me to do the little thing well.

My precious friend, as you read this book and hold it in your hands, humbly pray and commit to God that you will do the little thing well. Don't sit around for a lifetime waiting for God to ask you to do some *grand and glorious thing.*

I have met and studied the lives and even been privileged to be close to many great men and women of God. *They all have one thing in common no matter how great their exploits for God have been: they all started by doing the little thing well.*

Do the little thing well and it will lead to another little thing. And then to a little bigger thing and to something even bigger after that. One day, humble and content at your God-given task, the gentle flowing breeze of God's whispering wind will come and you will hear it. Promotion will call out your name.

7

It's Not Where You Start

The Kingdom of God is based upon increase. Where you start is not where you end up. Goodness, Mercy, and Increase will chase you all of the days of your life when promotion calls your name. Though your task now may be unseen and humble, never lose heart. *Be faithful and God will find you.* Your gift will make room for you and bring you before *great men.*

> A man's gift maketh room for him, and bringeth him before great men. (Proverbs 18:16)

If you are humble enough to start serving Jesus in places that a lot of folks would be too proud to, it will set into motion the *anointing of increase* in your life.

Big doors swing on little hinges. Doors that no man can shut will soon follow. Doors that anyone would like to have open in their lives. God's grace will tug on your heart to go through the small and seemingly insignificant door that man's pride would despise. Walk through it and be faithful—just because you love the Lord Jesus. It won't be the last door that you walk through. It's not where you start that matters most. God's *gravitational pull of promotion* is always onward and upward.

My Humble Beginnings

In the early years it seemed that my heart burned within me to preach, as it does today, but back then I couldn't buy a place to preach. Then, humble doors began to open.

Had you gone to a Kentucky shopping center, you would have seen a little tent at the edge of the parking lot. Cars driving past on the main highway, and even across the tarred pavement by the tent. People were talking, walking about, and unloading shopping carts.

Under the tent at 6:00 or 6:30 at night was an early tent service. Had you looked close, there were around 10 little grandmas and children. There was also a 16 year old boy whose ministry was just beginning.

The tiny little band of believers listened, and I'm not sure that they always listened intently to the 16 year old boy preach. It may not have been a big deal to them, but it sure was to him. I was that 16 year old boy and it was one of the biggest opportunities I ever had. It was life changing.

My whole world was being forever changed as I stood behind a tiny pulpit amid the noise of the traffic, the shoppers going by, the people who worked on the sound system, and the people setting up for the night's main event.

I didn't have that many sermons, but during the day I practiced my preaching and cried out to God to help me and to have mercy on me. It doesn't matter where you start.

Remember something: the next time you see someone starting and stepping out in what may be a *huge step* of faith for them, even though it may not look like a very big deal to you, *never discourage them! God's law of divine promotion will never leave them like you see them now. God may even use them to change the world.*

I remember the little building where I held my first revival, and it looked like an electrical building—the kind with a sign that says, "HIGH VOLTAGE. KEEP OUT." All that it lacked was the high fence and barbed wire around it. Dark as a dungeon inside, I preached to a scattered little handful.

Another little church I visited was heated with an old wood stove. Believe me that the fire fell one night and the church went from cold and in the 60s to what seemed like well-past 90 degrees. With a sweated brow, I labored there that night and rode out the heat of the burning wood inside the stove. It doesn't matter where you start.

There were places that Debbie and I stayed that were a little different. Precious people that were all unique and mostly very kind. A lot of them didn't have very much but they and God gave me a chance. I will always be eternally grateful for that.

Don't ever discourage a young person and especially someone just starting out. I hope that I never have. Please don't be critical of the young person who is just preaching their first sermons. Fan the flames of the preaching fire within them and don't ever say or do anything that would quench the flame. Once I was one of those young people just getting started. I was a flickering wick that God would not let go out. It doesn't matter where you start. Just start.

Not Small Forever

Start in humility and stay in humility. When the blessing comes and people begin to know your name, don't act like you pulled yourself up by your bootstraps. Don't ever give the self-made man or woman speech. If someone brags on you, simply brag on Jesus and say, "Thank God." We are called to be reflectors of the glory that God shines in and upon us.

You may start small but you will not stay

small. The work that you do today may be insignificant to man but it is not insignificant to God. Someone in Heaven is watching you and watching over you. Be faithful and pass the test. If you stumbled, fell, or quit, get back up right now and go right back to doing the last thing God told you to do.

Endure and even be cheerful during the proving ground. *God is most interested in laying a strong foundation in your life, for the coming prosperity and promotion that your Heavenly Father is going to bless you and your family with.*

God wants me to share with you one of the most important foundational stones:

Let God help you to be something for His glory even before you do something for His glory.

Choose to put this stone in the foundation of your life. Let God build your house upon this rock. Don't be like the shooting star that races across the heavenlies.

Do you want God to do something that matters for time and eternity with your life? Then let Jesus lay this cornerstone of *humility* in the foundation of your life.

Do You Want to Be Noticed by God?

When most people fail, it is not because they were not willing or able to do something big. It was because they were not humble enough to do the small things that lead to something big. Think about it.

If you go and look in Mother's Bible, you will find a very precious verse written in red.

Let this verse get in your spirit and be a guiding principle for your life:

> For whosoever exalteth himself shall be abased; and he that humbleth himself shall be exalted. (Luke 14:11)

We all live in a blow-your-own-horn-because-nobody-else-will world. But *blowing your own horn is not what gets you noticed by God or people*. Humility is. Jesus sat at the Pharisees' house and noticed how they jockeyed for the best seats in the best rooms with the most important people.

> Now He told a parable to those who were invited, [when] He noticed how

they were selecting the places of honor. (Luke 14:7 AMPC)

Then Jesus began to talk about how when you go to a wedding or supper, don't try to sit in the highest seat. Because if you do, someone else may come and you end up in the lowest room.

It might sound strange, but when I am out with a group or going to a restaurant, I always hold back or ask the host where they want me to sit. I've done the same thing at ministers' meetings and at all kinds of gatherings. I always end up with a good seat.

It is always best to be seated where the Lord has opened and made a way. God has a great seat reserved in your own name that nobody else will take. You don't have to elbow your way into a place at the King's table. A place setting is there with your name boldly printed, stating that this place is reserved for you. It may even be in the presence of your enemies.

The place that God has for you may be far above and beyond your own natural abilities, but it is your place in the spirit.

Follow the Holy Spirit's guidance and you will sit in a high place of God's choosing in the *rest* and *strength* of the *Lord Jesus Christ.*

It is not where you start in life or in ministry but where you end up that matters most. Even if nobody on earth ever knows your name, there is a day coming when you shall hear, "*Well done.*" Far better to be exalted for eternity than to have the temporary, fleeting, and fading glory of man.

Despise Not the Day of Small Things

Have you ever noticed how so many truly successful people started so very humbly? My Bible school president is a brilliant Bible teacher who has affected multiplied thousands for the Kingdom. Once, I heard him tell the story of when he and his precious wife graduated from Bible school. His classmates were going to exciting fields of ministry; some in his class were going to large churches and using their gifts and talents in very visible ways. But my future Bible school president had been led by God to stay and be the cook at the school where he and his wife graduated from.

After his classmates told him of their great opportunities, he remembers them asking him what his plans were. It was very humbling, and the devil—no doubt—told him that there was nothing great for him to do in ministry and he would never make it. But he made it all the way from being a cook in the kitchen, to leading a school for God.

If he had not been willing to do the humble task in the kitchen, he may never have been made Bible school president by the Lord.

Promotion will find you and call your name even in a kitchen. Promotion will have somebody find you when it looks like all of the world—and even the Church—have forgotten you and passed you by. Promotion doesn't pass anyone by that God wants promoted. It doesn't come from the east or the west. *Promotion* cometh from the Lord (Psalm 75:6).

Be faithful and God will find you.

Regularly I have listened intently and

heard great men and women of God tell me of their simple and very small beginnings. *God may give you a ministry that it seems no one else would ever want to do, but if you take the low seat and keep a good spirit, God may entrust you with a ministry that everyone would like to have.*

Humble people in line for a *promotion from the Lord* are willing to repetitively do over and over again the things that others won't.

I know a man who has a worldwide ministry and he still personally mows his mother's lawn. I know a pastor whose church is so big you could sit most of my childhood hometown in it. I have watched him—in another state far from his church, where no one could see—stoop over to pick up a piece of paper on the ground and put it in a trash can. I saw it and it preached to me.

Sometimes I will be pumping gas or at a hotel and I see paper and pick it up because of that man of God's example.

Little Obediences Lead to Big Blessings

If God can't get you to do a little thing well which no one ever sees, how on earth is He going to exalt you to do the great and big thing everybody will see?

Learn to do the little thing well in an obscure place where the eyes of man rarely look. It may be in a country field or in a bustling city. I have had Jesus send me to both. Humbly do your best, and do it not to impress anyone, but do it because you love the Lord.

A mighty general never starts out as a

general. But even a general is *always under authority*. Count it a privilege to be a foot soldier in the greatest army that has ever marched: the army of the Lord.

The one whose eye is on the sparrow is also lovingly watching over you. One day soon, those loving eyes will look in the direction of promotion and have promotion call your name.

8

The Ditch Anointing

Religion will pass you by if you are ever lying face-first and wounded on the ground in the ditch. Ditches are places that you don't ever want to be in.

I've seen some very precious people stumble into ditches. Only God's grace has kept me from lying face-first in a ditch right now and lost for all of eternity.

It is a great day when you receive revelation that God doesn't save you because of your own righteousness and the good deeds that you have done. Start with the fact that we all deserve to go to Hell forever and ever. The evil others have done could have easily been us without God's mercy and grace. The condescending Christian and the church that doesn't love the lost have entered the ecclesiastical ditch.

The day you start loving people only because Christ loves them and died for them and without wanting anything in return is a great day in your life. It is a day when promotion will call your name. The Lord will reward you openly for all you have done in secret.

After teaching on whoever humbles himself shall be exalted, Jesus immediately turned to His host and taught the people something else about when they make a dinner or a supper. *Jesus especially loves and invites people to dinner that nobody else loves or would invite.* We can still learn today from what He said about forgotten people:

> Then he turned to his host. "When you put on a luncheon or a banquet," he said, "don't invite your friends, brothers, relatives, and rich neighbors. For they will invite you back, and that will be your only reward. Instead, invite the poor, the crippled, the lame, and the blind. (Luke 14:12-13 NLT)

God is blessed when we bless people who can do nothing for us in the natural. Is it really ministry when you help someone so that they can do even more to help you in return? I think not.

Jesus replied with this story: "A man prepared a great feast and sent out many invitations. When the banquet was ready, he sent his servant to tell the guests, 'Come, the banquet is ready.' But they all began making excuses. One said, 'I have just bought a field and must inspect it. Please excuse me.' Another said, 'I have just bought five pairs of oxen, and I want to try them out. Please excuse me.' Another said, 'I just got married, so I can't come.' The servant returned and told his master what they had said. His master was furious and said, 'Go quickly into the streets and alleys of the town and invite the poor, the crippled, the blind, and the lame.' After the servant had done this, he reported, 'There is still room for more.' So his master said, 'Go out into the country lanes and behind the hedges and urge anyone you find to come, so that the house will be full. (Luke 14:16-23 NLT)

God Promotes Those Who Love Forgotten People

Where did they find all these people? They found them in the ditches and hurting places where they lay wounded and ignored as people passed them by every day.

A ditch is somewhere that you would not want to go in the natural.

If you were lying there cold, hungry, and hurting beneath the bushes, it must have felt so good to have someone see you and help you. There is a healing revival coming to the hedges of humanity. It is coming to the streets. A glorious message that there is a feast all prepared, and it is yours if you want to come and eat. The glorious refrain goes out into the highways and byways: "Come as you are. Come and sit at the table and you can receive."

Some people have a lot of excuses when it comes to doing the eternal things that really matter. But people in the ditch are hurting so badly that they don't really understand the excuses of those who could help them if they just would. They just want help. We really need to leave the padded theater seats where we worship on Sundays and go find them. The ditches are full of hurting people.

Debbie and I, as well as our entire family,

have dedicated our lives to going and reaching out to a lost world that is going to Hell. As we go out, we do not go in our name, but we go to lift up the strong name of Jesus. It is the name that heals all of the hurts of humanity.

Don't Waste Your Life

Jesus is still waiting for you to go. The Word plainly tells us what to do and how to do it. It does not have to be theorized or sent back to a committee for further review. We just need to go. We need to go to the ditches where the lost and suffering lie. *I will not spend my life at a banquet for the saved*. I must be excused. I have an appointment with the lost. A divine appointment.

The cry from the ditch compels me to go. I've heard blind Bartimaeus call. I've seen the harvest. I cannot stay with "church as usual."

The ditches of hurting humanity are so full. People nearly trip over them while on their way to church. Divorced and abandoned mothers line the ditches on roads. The paroled prisoner who struggles to get a job and has almost given up is in that ditch. Poor children with clothes that are not as good as others' are there. Sad and dejected dads who struggle with sin and can't provide for their families are in the lineup. Forgotten old people with stories to tell and nobody to listen sit in silence and are negligently passed by. Human shipwrecks from alcohol, opioids, and other drugs watch the church people pass on by. Others are proud but hurting, bleeding silently within and hoping that no one notices they have a problem.

Why do we ever sit half-asleep in half-empty churches? Let's empty out the half that are there in God's house and send them to the byways and the ditches.

What if this message was preached: "Don't come back here until you bring someone from the ditch"? Someone hurting so badly that you have to almost, or even literally, carry them into God's house. Put your arm around someone bleeding in the city or country town where you live and take them to the feast. *Wherever the Word is preached, it is a feast where every seat should be full.*

Many of you will have something happen

as soon as you kneel by the suffering. Your healing moment physically, and even spiritually, will arrive right there in the ditch. You will never be the same, and peace will come.

What gives God joy gives me strength. You will never again be satisfied with a life that doesn't involve doing something eternal. The ditches of this world need to be empty. The churches need to be full. The approving eyes of Jesus still gaze upon and watch over His children who love those who have been forgotten.

When you are loving God by loving His people, you will do something for someone that no one else sees or knows about. *You won't care that no one else sees or knows about what you have done.* It is then that promotion calls your name.

When *He who made the heavens* calls your name, your life—which is not your own—will never be the same.

I have prayed for you, that as you read this book, God would enlarge your borders and exalt you on high. I have asked God to give you influence, possessions, and a great name in Heaven and on earth. I only ask, in the name of the One who sent me, that *the higher God lifts you up, and the more He gives you, the more you will do for the Kingdom.*

Greatness is not really greatness if it doesn't involve something eternal for Jesus. Heaven and earth are passing away, but that which is done for Christ will never pass away.

A moment of God's favor is worth more than a lifetime of self-effort. Spend and invest your life on that which is eternal.

Promoted People Have Been Taught

One day an expert in religious law stood up to test Jesus by asking him this question: "Teacher, what should I do to inherit eternal life?" Jesus replied, "What does the law of Moses say? How do you read it?" The man answered, "'You must love the Lord your God with all your heart, all your soul, all your strength, and all your mind.' And, 'Love your neighbor as yourself.'" "Right!" Jesus told him. "Do this and you will live!" The man wanted to justify his actions, so he asked Jesus, "And who is my neighbor?" "Jesus replied with a story: "A Jewish man was traveling from

Jerusalem down to Jericho, and he was attacked by bandits…" (Luke 10:25-30 NLT)

When the lawyer, trying to justify himself, said to Jesus, "And who is my neighbor?" (verse 29), Jesus gave an answer for the ages. The sarcastic lawyer prompted Jesus to tell one of the greatest stories that have ever been told (the story of the Good Samaritan). All the while, the twelve were listening.

Jesus taught them all to go into the ditches of this world. To love all people, regardless of their skin color or background. To love hurting and forgotten people the world has thrown away. *Everybody is somebody to Jesus.*

Remember this: *the twelve were taught.* We sure need more teaching on loving those who lie bleeding and dying in the ditches of this world. A church that is too dignified to help the hurting is preaching a gospel that Jesus never taught.

Obedience to the Word brings supernatural blessing. You must be a doer of the Word, not just a hearer of the Word.

Find your ditch. This is what Jesus taught the twelve. The teaching is still true today. It will still bear eternal fruit today.

Money Follows Ministry

If you really want to help people get up out of the ditch, you will never lack money. You will always have silver to give to the innkeeper. You will say, "Take care of this person from the ditch, and if this is not enough. I will give you more." Your business will be blessed. Your children will be blessed. Your ministry will be blessed. Since I started loving people in the ditch, I have never lacked a place to preach. Neither will you.

It hurts to say this, but sometimes the ditch is a padded pew within the walls of a high steeple and stained glass. Sometimes the ditch is charismatic and sings with great fervor, but with talents not used to win the lost. Their worship does not exalt *Christ* and the *finished work* that He completed upon the cross. The skillful music has become entertainment for the crowd.

It only takes a few years of mission drift, and a church isn't even a church anymore; at least not a *New Testament church* focused on winning the lost and the *soon coming of Jesus*.

We need Jesus to teach us, and teach us soon, through anointed men and women of God. The end of the world is at hand. The night cometh when no man can work.

Will you go into the field and let our Heavenly Father promote you for *His purposes*? There is one more *revival* coming, and even as a nation was born in a day, a river of forgiveness and mercy will flow. Millions—whole nations—will be swept into the Kingdom. Let the Church awaken and arise in Christ's Love.

The Teachable Church

Wherever the Word is untaught, people's lives will stay unchanged. But a spirit-empowered word, taught to a faith-filled church will change the world for God. It will also empty the ditches and hurting places, populate Heaven, and make it hard for people to go to Hell.

When the Church empties out to evangelize the ditch, God's house will be full. Full of people once in the ditch themselves who know how to win souls for Jesus Christ. The nearby ditch is where almost every worldwide ministry begins.

In Luke 10:27, Jesus taught that you must "love the Lord your God with all your heart and with all your soul and with all your strength and with all your mind; *and your neighbor as yourself*" (AMPC). As we already know, in verse 29, when the attorney asks, "And who is my neighbor?" Jesus took us for a trip on the Jericho Road. *Your neighbor is the one near you who has a need and is hurting.* A relationship that reaches vertically to God always reaches out horizontally to your neighbor. *A heavenly experience that does not manifest itself in ministry isn't worth all that much.* Stay in the prayer room, but leave it often to go to the ditch where the sick, sinful, suffering, and in need of ministry lie.

A lot of preachers parse Greek verbs in their offices and debate doctrine. Others love to study doctrinal theoretics, yet walk on past the hurting who lie silent and in pain on the side of the road. They have become the Levite who walked right on by the wounded man who lay suffering on the Jericho Road.

9

Promoted by Invisible Ministry

Real ministry is often done where and when no one else sees. It is often done one-on-one and far away from the crowd. It is done where the dust and dirt are. But it is always seen by all-seeing eyes.

Often, ministry that no one on earth sees is the very most effective. It will also get you promoted faster than anything else. You're not working to get promoted. You're just being faithful because you love the Lord. But that's usually when promotion will come out of nowhere and change your life forever. You minister in obscurity with a heart that is full and running over with God's love. Then it happens: God shines His *light* on you and *favor* and *promotion* come to stay in your life forever— forever so you can keep loving God and loving people. You can be forever blessed and go from glory to glory, by God's grace, as you love what God loves and help those God leads you to help.

In Luke 10:36-37, the lawyer's destiny hung in the balances. He could be a Good Samaritan and help the people that he passed by who were hurting and in need, or he could just pass them by.

"Now which of these three would you say was a neighbor to the man who was attacked by bandits?" Jesus asked. The man replied, "The one who showed him mercy." Then Jesus said, "Yes, now go and do the same." (Luke 10:36-37 NLT)

As the lawyer's destiny hung in the balances, so does yours.

When you pass by the people that Jesus wants you to love and help, you are passing up a wonderful life. If you will love what God loves, He will promote you. If you will promote *His* cause of winning the lost to Jesus, you will be promoted on high. If you will spend your money on that which is eternal, God will fill your basket and storehouse until it runs over.

Your future depends on how you treat your neighbor. The sarcastic lawyer had very little of a future if he did not learn who his neighbor was. You can't be blessed spending your life passing people in the ditch.

Start with whatever you have to work with wherever you are. Bless your neighbor across the lawn and someday God may have you go to a neighboring nation.

Lepers Left to Die

I believe in divine connections and I believe in divine opportunities. You are the judge and the jury in the courtroom of your destiny. You decide. Heaven and your neighbor await your verdict.

It's time to stop ignoring the hurting and walking by on the other side of the road. How many people has religion left on the other side of the road? How many sick people come to church and are left still in the ditch? How many people have never been delivered from sexual sin and taught how to stay delivered, but are labeled as lepers and left to die? That's not how Jesus treated the woman taken in the very act of adultery. Prostitutes and lepers, along with the maniac from the country of the Gadarenes, would all say the same thing about Jesus: "He stopped and healed me when no one else would."

God is bigger than your hang-up. Bigger than your problem. Bigger than a church split. Bigger than your backsliding. *There is no ditch so deep that Jesus cannot get to the bottom of it.*

One defining moment in the presence of

Jesus will set you free from a meaningless life. Jesus will set you free from sin, and Jesus will set you free from yourself. *If you really want to start living, start loving people and helping people.* Start by serving your own family. Start with what is in your hand. *Do the little thing well,* and promotion will start to chase you.

Start looking. Start seeing—really seeing. Don't cross the road to the other side and ignore the hurting that is all around you.

The Cold and Windy City

The Jesus in you wants to stop. Not stop and stare. Not stop and criticize. But stop and be a blessing. That's what real compassion is.

In the downtown area of the windy city of

Chicago, on a cold night many years ago, I saw something that touched my heart. It still stirs me just to write and talk about it.

As I rode in a car with a pastor on a busy street, I could see a precious woman sitting on the sidewalk, with her back up against the wall of a building. People passed her by as if she were invisible. She was nameless and never even given a second thought by the crowd.

The lady was covered by a blanket, and it was so cold that night late in the year. It was then that I saw a sight that I could never forget. It touched my soul deep within me: I could see two other little feet sticking out from underneath the blanket.

Here was a precious woman who had her child and was sleeping on a cold sidewalk. Covered by just a blanket in one of the great cities of America. Cradling her child between her legs, trying to keep her little one warm.

I still wonder if I should have implored the pastor to stop. It all happened in a flash as quickly as I glanced out the window of a moving vehicle. But I never will forget her, and I pray that I did not leave someone hurting on the Jericho Road of downtown Chicago.

There is a Jericho Road in every city, in every town, and in every village. The wounded, the poor, and the suffering are there. Don't pass them by. Don't cross onto the other side of the street like you don't see them. Love and encourage those who are just getting started in their dreams. Someone helped you. When God raises you up and promotion calls your name, never forget where you came from and how far you have come *by the grace of God.*

The Neighborhood That People Forgot

In 1939, if you had been walking down Franklin Street, on the edge of Tampa, Florida, you most likely would have wanted to leave. Sin and alcohol which travel together had pretty well destroyed the neighborhood. It was a poor ghetto, where pretty much anyone who could leave, had left.

The people who lived there were suffering, and the enemy—the devil—had stolen just about everything anybody had, including their dignity. It was ditch where precious people who had been wounded, beat up, and left behind on the Jericho Road of life, lay in plain sight.

It was a world ignored by most, and rarely visited by anyone, with only those who felt they had to be there. But in 1939, if you had walked in that hurting and poor neighborhood, you would have heard a voice. Not the voice of an angel (because I doubt angels would have slightly southern accents), but voice in the ditch on the Jericho Road of life named Franklin Street told *good news*.

It wasn't an eloquent voice. It could not have been fancy even if it wanted to be. *But good news doesn't have to be eloquently told*. The voice had been dedicated and yielded to God in prayer.

No one else wanted to hear him preach, and there were no other open doors for the 21 year old Bible school student. So he preached his first sermons to precious souls who lay hurting in a spiritual ditch, and maybe even a literal one, on Franklin Street.

The world took little notice. No crowds came. No great newspaper printed front page accounts of what was said. Did anyone really listen? Did anyone respond, or even care? As the 21 year old beginning preacher did his best to sow the seed of God's Word on mighty hard soil, only eternity will tell what the results, if any, were.

Was the precious young man discouraged? Maybe. Maybe the enemy told him that he didn't *really* have what it took to preach the glorious Gospel of good news. We may never really know. What I do know is this: I'm so glad the tall and skinny preacher didn't quit and give up. Heaven heard and Heaven saw and *divine promotion called his name*.

His name was William Graham, and all of his friends called him Billy.

Remember: *where you start is not where you end up* when *divine promotion* comes into your life and calls your name.

Some 40 years later, on the last night of the Tampa, Florida Crusade, over 52,000 people attended. God, do it again.

God's *divine promotion* looks in little places for unnoticed people who have the heart of the Good Samaritan. *Then, He calls their name and does for them—with them—what no power on earth could ever do.*

The place called Franklin Street, a little neighborhood on the edge the major city of Tampa, is still mostly forgotten even today. But if you go there, you will see a green historical marker that is starting to age.

This is what it says:

"From the sidewalk in this Franklin St. neighborhood, the Rev. Dr. Billy Graham forty years ago launched his worldwide Christian evangelistic crusade, exhorting derelicts, drunks and 'Skid Row' bums. Since then he has preached to more people than any other person, reaching millions. Dr. Graham attended Florida Bible Institute at Temple Terrace, graduating in 1940. While a student here, Dr. Graham heard the 'call', and prayed, 'O God, if you want me to preach, I will do it'.

"Erected in 1979 by the TAMPA HISTORICAL SOCIETY in cooperation with the TAMPA MINISTERS' ASSOCIATION during the Billy Graham Crusade in Tampa."

Be faithful and God will find you. Love God, and love people, especially the ones who can never pay you back. Heaven sees what no one else sees, and remembers what man forgets.

One day soon, the *sweetest voice* that you have ever heard, will call you by name. Listen and obey the call of that voice. It will cause you to go where no man, but only *Jesus,* can take you. A place of *divine promotion, in this life, for all of time, and for e t e r n i t y.*

Pray this prayer to ask Jesus into your heart and be saved for all of eternity:

Heavenly Father, in Jesus' name, please forgive me for all of my sin. I believe that You are the true Son of God, and I claim Your shed blood on the cross of Calvary to pay for my sins. Wash me clean from all of my sins, and I will serve You the rest of my life. One day, I want to go to Heaven and live with You forever.

Made in the USA
Middletown, DE
22 March 2019